Photo Anthology

CROATIA LIFE

Robbie Orbit

Copyright © 2019 by Robbie. Orbit
All rights reserved. This book or any portion thereof
may not be reproduced or used in any manner whatsoever
without the express written permission of the publisher
except for the use of brief quotations in a book review.
ISBN:978-1-67818-041-6

IF THE CITY'S PARKS AND GARDENS ARE HAVENS OF TRANQUILLITY, ZAGREB'S SQUARES, WHEN NOT OCCUPIED BY GARDENS, ARE PLACES WHERE THE CITY'S HEARTBEATS ARE HEARD THE LOUDEST.

ANITA RAO-KASHI

"TRAVEL IS FATAL TO PREJUDICE, BIGOTRY, AND NARROW MINDEDNESS, AND MANY OF OUR PEOPLE NEED IT SORELY ON THESE ACCOUNTS."
MARK TWAIN

"THE WORLD IS A BOOK AND THOSE WHO DO NOT TRAVEL READ ONLY A PAGE."
SAINT AUGUSTINE.

"LIVE WITH NO EXCUSES AND TRAVEL WITH NO REGRETS"
OSCAR WILDE.

"Not all those who wander are lost"
J.R.R. Tolkien

"Life is either a daring adventure or nothing at all."
Helen Keller